Table of Content

Table of Content..1
Bison stew..4
Fry bread..6
Wild rice casserole...8
Three sisters soup (corn, beans, squash) 10
Cedar-planked salmon...12
Blue corn pancakes..14
Venison jerky 16
Navajo tacos..18
Acorn squash with maple glaze 20
Pemmican (dried meat and berries) 22
Green chile stew..24
Elk chili..26
Huckleberry pie 28
Rabbit stew...30
Indian pudding (cornmeal pudding) 32
Acorn bread..34
Smoked trout..36
Sunchoke soup..38
Maple sugar candy..40
Bear stew 42
Wild mushroom risotto...44

Cranberry sauce 46

Rabbit fry 48

Deer jerky 50

Cornbread stuffing 52

Juniper berry roasted quail 54

Sweet potato casserole 56

Elk burgers 58

Succotash (corn and lima beans) 60

Blueberry muffins 62

Bison meatloaf 64

Purslane salad 66

Salmon cakes 68

Elk stew 70

Pumpkin soup 72

Maple glazed carrots 74

Wild rice salad 76

Sunflower seed bread 78

Buffalo burgers 80

Indian tacos 82

Blackberry cobbler 84

Elk steak 86

Corn fritters 88

Sassafras tea 90

Maple bacon 92

Wild greens salad 94

Bison ribs 96

Sunflower seed butter cookies 98

Wild onion soup 100

Elk roast 102

Acorn squash soup 104

Blueberry pancakes 106

Bison roast 108

Parsnip mash 110

Duck confit 112

Maple roasted turnips 114

Wild rice porridge 116

Squash soup 118

Bison chili 120

Bison stew

Ingredients:

- 1 lb Bison meat
- 1 onion
- 2 carrots
- 2 potatoes
- 4 cups beef broth
- 1 tsp thyme
- Salt & pepper to taste

Equipment:

1. Knife
2. Cutting board
3. Pot
4. Stirring spoon
5. Dutch oven

Methods:

Step 1: Heat olive oil in a large pot over medium heat.
Step 2: Add diced onions, celery, and carrots to the pot and sauté until the vegetables are soft.
Step 3: Season bison meat with salt and pepper, then add it to the pot.
Step 4: Brown the meat on all sides, stirring occasionally.
Step 5: Stir in crushed tomatoes, beef broth, and herbs like thyme and rosemary.
Step 6: Cover the pot and let the stew simmer for about 2 hours, until the meat is tender.

Step 7: Adjust seasoning with salt and pepper before serving. Enjoy your delicious bison stew!

Helpful Tips:

1. Start by browning the bison meat in a hot pan to enhance flavor.
2. Use a mix of vegetables like carrots, onions, and celery for added depth of flavor.
3. Consider adding herbs like thyme, rosemary, and bay leaves for a rich taste profile.
4. Use a beef or bison broth as the base for the stew for a more intense flavor.
5. Cook on low heat for a longer period of time to allow the meat to become tender.
6. Taste and adjust seasoning as necessary throughout the cooking process.
7. Serve with a side of crusty bread or mashed potatoes for a complete meal.

Fry bread

Ingredients:

- 2 cups all-purpose flour
- 1 tablespoon baking powder
- 1 teaspoon salt
- 1 cup warm water

Equipment:

1. Mixing bowl
2. Rolling pin
3. Skillet
4. Tongs
5. Knife
6. Cutting board

Methods:

Step 1: In a large mixing bowl, combine 2 cups of flour, 1 tablespoon of baking powder, and a pinch of salt.
Step 2: Gradually add 3/4 cup of warm water, mixing until a dough forms.
Step 3: Knead the dough on a floured surface for 5 minutes, then let it rest for 10 minutes.
Step 4: Heat vegetable oil in a large skillet over medium-high heat.
Step 5: Divide the dough into 4 equal pieces and flatten each into a disk.
Step 6: Fry each disk in the hot oil until golden brown, about 2-3 minutes per side.
Step 7: Serve warm and enjoy!

Helpful Tips:

1. Always use fresh ingredients for the best flavor.
2. Make sure your oil is hot enough before adding the dough to prevent it from absorbing too much oil.
3. Use a high-quality flour for better texture and taste.
4. Knead the dough well to ensure it is smooth and elastic.
5. Let the dough rest before rolling it out to relax the gluten and make it easier to work with.
6. Roll out the dough evenly to ensure it cooks evenly.
7. Fry the bread in small batches to prevent overcrowding the pan.
8. Drain the fried bread on paper towels to remove excess oil before serving.
9. Enjoy your fry bread while it's still hot and fresh!

Wild rice casserole

Ingredients:

- 1 cup wild rice
- 2 cups chicken broth
- 1/2 cup chopped onion
- 1/2 cup sliced mushrooms
- 1/4 cup chopped parsley
- 1/4 cup shredded cheese

Equipment:

1. Cutting board
2. Chef's knife
3. Mixing bowls
4. Casserole dish
5. Mixing spoon
6. Pot or saucepan

Methods:

Step 1: Preheat the oven to 350°F.
Step 2: Cook 1 cup of wild rice according to package instructions.
Step 3: In a large skillet, sauté 1 diced onion and 2 cloves of minced garlic in olive oil until softened.
Step 4: Add 1 diced bell pepper and 1 diced carrot to the skillet and cook until slightly tender.
Step 5: Stir in 1 can of diced tomatoes, 1 cup of vegetable broth, and the cooked wild rice.
Step 6: Season with salt, pepper, and dried herbs of your choice.
Step 7: Transfer the mixture to a baking dish and bake for 25-30 minutes.
Step 8: Serve hot and enjoy your wild rice casserole!

Helpful Tips:

1. Cook the wild rice according to package instructions before adding to the casserole.
2. Use a combination of vegetables like mushrooms, bell peppers, and carrots for added flavor and texture.
3. Consider adding protein like chicken, turkey, or tofu to make the dish more filling.
4. Opt for low-sodium broth to control the salt level in the casserole.
5. Mix in herbs like thyme, rosemary, or sage for aromatic depth.
6. Top the casserole with a blend of cheeses for a gooey, flavorful finish.
7. Bake the casserole covered with foil to prevent the top layer from drying out.

Three sisters soup (corn, beans, squash)

Ingredients:

- 1 can of corn
- 1 can of black beans
- 1 butternut squash
- 1 onion
- 1 bell pepper
- 4 cups of vegetable broth

Equipment:

1. Knife
2. Cutting board
3. Saucepan
4. Wooden spoon
5. Mixing bowl

Methods:

Step 1: Start by gathering all the ingredients: corn, beans, squash, onions, bell peppers, garlic, tomatoes, and vegetable broth.
Step 2: In a large pot, sauté the onions, bell peppers, and garlic until they are soft.
Step 3: Add the corn, beans, and squash to the pot and stir well to combine.
Step 4: Pour in the vegetable broth and bring the soup to a boil.
Step 5: Reduce the heat and let the soup simmer for about 20 minutes, until the vegetables are cooked through.
Step 6: Season with salt, pepper, and any other desired spices.
Step 7: Serve hot and enjoy your delicious three sisters soup!

Helpful Tips:

1. Start by sautéing onion, garlic, and bell peppers in a large pot.
2. Add diced butternut squash and cook until slightly softened.
3. Stir in canned black beans and corn, along with vegetable broth and diced tomatoes.
4. Season with salt, pepper, cumin, and paprika for extra flavor.
5. Let the soup simmer for at least 20 minutes to allow the flavors to meld together.
6. Consider adding kale or spinach for added nutrients.
7. Serve hot and garnish with fresh cilantro or avocado slices.
8. Enjoy with cornbread or tortilla chips on the side.

Cedar-planked salmon

Ingredients:

- 4 salmon fillets
- 1 cedar plank
- 1 lemon
- 4 tbsp olive oil
- Salt and pepper

Equipment:

1. Grill
2. Tongs
3. Spatula
4. Basting brush
5. Kitchen shears

Methods:

Step 1: Soak cedar plank in water for at least 1 hour.
Step 2: Preheat grill to medium-high heat.
Step 3: Place salmon fillets on cedar plank, skin-side down.
Step 4: Season salmon with salt, pepper, and any desired herbs or spices.
Step 5: Place cedar plank with salmon on grill and cover.
Step 6: Cook salmon for about 15-20 minutes, or until it flakes easily with a fork.
Step 7: Remove cedar plank from grill and let salmon rest for a few minutes.
Step 8: Serve salmon directly on cedar plank or transfer to a serving platter.
Step 9: Enjoy your delicious cedar-planked salmon!

Helpful Tips:

1. Soak the cedar plank in water for at least 1-2 hours before cooking to prevent it from catching on fire.
2. Preheat your grill before placing the plank with salmon on top to ensure even cooking.
3. Season the salmon with your favorite herbs, spices, and a drizzle of olive oil before placing it on the plank.
4. Place the cedar-planked salmon on the grill over indirect heat to cook it slowly and prevent it from burning.
5. Keep a spray bottle of water nearby in case the plank starts to flame up during cooking.
6. Use a meat thermometer to ensure the salmon reaches an internal temperature of 145°F before serving.

Blue corn pancakes

Ingredients:

- 1 cup blue cornmeal
- 1/2 cup all-purpose flour
- 1 tbsp baking powder
- 1/4 tsp salt
- 1 1/4 cups milk
- 1 egg
- 2 tbsp butter, melted

Equipment:

1. Mixing bowl
2. Whisk
3. Skillet
4. Spatula
5. Ladle

Methods:

Step 1: In a mixing bowl, combine 1 cup of blue cornmeal, 1 cup of all-purpose flour, 2 tablespoons of sugar, 1 tablespoon of baking powder, and 1/2 teaspoon of salt.
Step 2: In a separate bowl, whisk together 1 1/2 cups of milk, 2 eggs, and 3 tablespoons of melted butter.
Step 3: Pour the wet ingredients into the dry ingredients and stir until just combined.
Step 4: Heat a non-stick skillet over medium heat and lightly grease with butter.
Step 5: Pour 1/4 cup of batter onto the skillet for each pancake and cook until bubbles form on the surface.
Step 6: Flip and cook for another 2-3 minutes until golden brown.

Step 7: Serve hot with maple syrup and butter. Enjoy your delicious blue corn pancakes!

Helpful Tips:

1. Use blue cornmeal for an authentic flavor and color.
2. Mix the batter until just combined to avoid tough pancakes.
3. Let the batter rest for 10-15 minutes before cooking to allow the flavors to meld.
4. Cook pancakes on a medium-low heat to prevent burning.
5. Add in your favorite mix-ins like blueberries or chocolate chips for an extra kick.
6. Serve hot with butter and maple syrup for a delicious breakfast treat.

Venison jerky

Ingredients:

- 1 lb venison
- 1/4 cup soy sauce
- 2 tbsp Worcestershire sauce
- 1 tsp garlic powder
- 1 tsp black pepper

Equipment:

1. Knife
2. Cutting board
3. Mixing bowl
4. Baking sheet
5. Oven
6. Food dehydrator

Methods:

Step 1: Start by cutting the venison into thin strips, about ¼ inch thick.
Step 2: In a bowl, mix together soy sauce, worcestershire sauce, honey, garlic powder, onion powder, black pepper, and liquid smoke.
Step 3: Place the venison strips in the marinade and let them sit for at least 4 hours, preferably overnight.
Step 4: Preheat your oven to 175°F (80°C) and line a baking sheet with foil.
Step 5: Lay the marinated venison strips on the baking sheet in a single layer.
Step 6: Bake for 3-4 hours, or until the jerky is dry and firm.
Step 7: Allow the jerky to cool before storing in an airtight container. Enjoy your homemade venison jerky!

Helpful Tips:

1. Use lean cuts of venison, such as the hindquarter or backstraps, for the best jerky results.
2. Trim off any excess fat and silver skin before slicing the meat into thin strips.
3. Marinate the venison in a combination of soy sauce, Worcestershire sauce, and your favorite seasonings for at least 4 hours or overnight.
4. Preheat your oven to the lowest temperature setting (usually around 170°F) or use a dehydrator for even drying.
5. Place the marinated venison strips on wire racks or baking sheets and dry for 4-6 hours, turning halfway through.
6. Store the jerky in an airtight container for up to one month. Enjoy as a tasty and protein-packed snack!

Navajo tacos

Ingredients:

- 2 cups flour
- 1 tsp baking powder
- 1/2 tsp salt
- 3/4 cup warm water
- 1 lb ground beef
- 1 onion
- 1 can diced tomatoes
- Shredded lettuce

Equipment:

1. Spatula
2. Whisk
3. Knife
4. Cutting Board
5. Skillet

Methods:

Step 1: In a mixing bowl, combine 2 cups of flour, 1 teaspoon of salt, and 1 tablespoon of baking powder.
Step 2: Slowly add ¾ cup of warm water to the flour mixture, stirring until a dough forms.
Step 3: Knead the dough on a floured surface for a few minutes until smooth.
Step 4: Divide the dough into 6 equal portions and flatten each into a disk.
Step 5: Heat oil in a skillet over medium-high heat.
Step 6: Fry each disk of dough in the hot oil until golden brown and cooked through.
Step 7: Top with your favorite taco ingredients and enjoy your Navajo tacos!

Helpful Tips:

1. Start by making your own fry bread using a simple dough of flour, baking powder, salt, and water.
2. Roll out the dough into small rounds and fry in hot oil until golden brown on both sides.
3. Cook up some ground beef or shredded chicken with your favorite taco seasoning for the meat topping.
4. Don't forget to prepare all the toppings like shredded lettuce, diced tomatoes, cheese, and sour cream.
5. Assemble your Navajo tacos by placing the fry bread on a plate and topping with the cooked meat and toppings.
6. Enjoy your delicious homemade Navajo tacos!

Acorn squash with maple glaze

Ingredients:

- 2 acorn squash
- 1/4 cup maple syrup
- 2 tbsp olive oil
- Salt and pepper to taste

Equipment:

1. Knife
2. Cutting board
3. Baking sheet
4. Mixing bowl
5. Whisk
6. Brush

Methods:

Step 1: Preheat the oven to 400°F.
Step 2: Cut the acorn squash in half and scoop out the seeds.
Step 3: Place the squash halves cut-side down on a baking sheet.
Step 4: Roast in the oven for 30-40 minutes, or until the squash is soft.
Step 5: While the squash is roasting, mix together maple syrup, melted butter, cinnamon, and a pinch of salt in a small bowl.
Step 6: Remove the squash from the oven and flip them over.
Step 7: Brush the maple glaze over the squash halves.
Step 8: Return to the oven for 5-10 minutes, until the glaze is bubbly.
Step 9: Serve hot and enjoy!

Helpful Tips:

1. Preheat oven to 400°F.
2. Cut acorn squash in half, scoop out seeds, and slice into 1-inch wedges.
3. Place squash on a baking sheet lined with parchment paper.
4. In a small bowl, mix together maple syrup, melted butter, and a pinch of salt.
5. Brush maple glaze onto each squash wedge.
6. Roast in the oven for about 25-30 minutes, or until squash is tender and caramelized.
7. Optional: sprinkle with chopped nuts or dried cranberries before serving.
8. Enjoy your delicious and nutritious maple glazed acorn squash!

Pemmican (dried meat and berries)

Ingredients:

- 1 lb dried meat strips
- 1/2 cup dried berries
- 4 tbsp rendered fat

Equipment:

1. Knife
2. Cutting board
3. Skillet
4. Oven
5. Mixing bowl

Methods:

Step 1: Gather necessary ingredients - lean meat, berries, and rendered fat.
Step 2: Slice the meat into thin strips and dry thoroughly.
Step 3: Grind the dried meat into a powder.
Step 4: Crush the berries into a powder.
Step 5: Mix the meat powder and berry powder together in a bowl.
Step 6: Slowly add rendered fat to the mixture until it forms a paste.
Step 7: Shape the paste into small, round patties or bars.
Step 8: Let the pemmican dry and harden for a few days before storing in a cool, dry place.
Step 9: Enjoy as a nutritious and delicious snack for hiking or camping!

Helpful Tips:

1. Start by dehydrating lean cuts of meat, such as beef or venison, until they are completely dry.

2. Pound the dried meat into a fine powder using a mortar and pestle or a food processor.
3. Add in dried berries, such as cranberries or blueberries, to the powdered meat.
4. Mix in rendered fat, such as tallow or lard, to bind the mixture together.
5. Shape the mixture into small patties or bars and allow them to cool and harden.
6. Store the pemmican in a cool, dry place or vacuum-sealed bags for long-term preservation.
7. Enjoy as a nutritious and portable snack on your next outdoor adventure.

Green chile stew

Ingredients:

- 2 lbs pork, cubed
- 2 cups green chile
- 1 onion, diced
- 4 cloves garlic, minced
- 4 cups chicken broth
- 2 potatoes, diced
- Salt and pepper to taste

Equipment:

1. Cutting board
2. Knife
3. Pot
4. Wooden spoon
5. Ladle

Methods:

Step 1: Heat oil in a large pot over medium heat.
Step 2: Add diced onions and sauté until translucent.
Step 3: Stir in minced garlic and cook for another minute.
Step 4: Add diced green chiles, chopped potatoes, and chicken broth.
Step 5: Bring to a boil, then reduce heat and let simmer for 20 minutes.
Step 6: Stir in diced tomatoes, cooked shredded chicken, and season with salt and pepper.
Step 7: Simmer for another 10 minutes until potatoes are tender.
Step 8: Serve hot with tortillas or over rice.
Step 9: Enjoy your delicious green chile stew!

Helpful Tips:

1. Start by roasting your green chiles over an open flame or in the oven until charred. This will bring out their flavor and add a smoky element to your stew.
2. Use a variety of meats, such as pork, beef, or chicken, to add depth of flavor to your stew.
3. Don't forget to include potatoes, onions, and garlic for added texture and flavor.
4. Consider adding beans, such as pinto or black beans, for an extra dose of protein and heartiness.
5. Season your stew with a combination of spices like cumin, oregano, and coriander for a well-rounded taste.
6. Serve your green chile stew with warm tortillas or rice for a complete meal. Enjoy!

Elk chili

Ingredients:

- 1 lb ground elk
- 1 can red kidney beans
- 1 can diced tomatoes
- 1 onion, diced
- 1 green bell pepper, diced
- 2 cloves garlic, minced
- Chili powder, cumin, salt, and pepper to taste

Equipment:

1. Cutting board
2. Chef's knife
3. Wooden spoon
4. Saucepan
5. Ladle

Methods:

Step 1: In a large pot, heat oil over medium heat.
Step 2: Add chopped onions and garlic, cook until onions are soft.
Step 3: Add ground elk meat and brown, breaking it up with a wooden spoon.
Step 4: Stir in chili powder, cumin, paprika, and salt.
Step 5: Pour in diced tomatoes, tomato sauce, and beef broth.
Step 6: Bring to a simmer, then reduce heat and let it cook for 1-2 hours.
Step 7: Add drained kidney beans and simmer for another 30 minutes.
Step 8: Serve hot with toppings like shredded cheese and sour cream.
Enjoy your elk chili!

Helpful Tips:

1. Use lean ground elk meat for a healthier option.
2. Brown the meat before adding it to the chili for added flavor.
3. Consider mixing in some spicy peppers for extra heat.
4. Don't forget to add in plenty of beans for texture and protein.
5. Use a variety of herbs and spices to enhance the flavor profile.
6. Consider adding in some dark chocolate for a unique twist.
7. Let the chili simmer on low heat for at least an hour to allow the flavors to meld together.
8. Serve with your favorite toppings like shredded cheese, sour cream, and fresh cilantro.

Huckleberry pie

Ingredients:

- 2 cups fresh huckleberries
- 1/2 cup sugar
- 2 tbsp cornstarch
- 1 tbsp lemon juice
- 1/4 tsp cinnamon
- 1 pie crust

Equipment:

1. Mixing bowl
2. Rolling pin
3. Pie dish
4. Pastry brush
5. Pie server

Methods:

Step 1: Preheat the oven to 375°F.
Step 2: Roll out pie dough and place it in a pie dish.
Step 3: In a mixing bowl, combine huckleberries, sugar, cornstarch, lemon juice, and cinnamon.
Step 4: Pour the huckleberry mixture into the pie crust.
Step 5: Roll out the second pie dough and place it on top of the pie.
Step 6: Crimp the edges of the pie crust to seal in the filling.
Step 7: Cut slits in the top crust to allow steam to escape.
Step 8: Brush the top crust with egg wash and sprinkle with sugar.
Step 9: Bake the pie for 45-50 minutes, or until the crust is golden brown.
Step 10: Allow the pie to cool before serving. Enjoy your delicious huckleberry pie!

Helpful Tips:

1. Use fresh huckleberries for the best flavor.
2. Rinse the huckleberries thoroughly before using them in the pie.
3. Mix the huckleberries with sugar, lemon juice, and cornstarch for a thick filling.
4. Use a double crust for the pie, either homemade or store-bought.
5. Brush the crust with an egg wash before baking for a golden finish.
6. Make slits in the top crust to allow steam to escape during baking.
7. Bake the pie at a higher temperature initially, then lower the heat to ensure a fully cooked crust and filling.
8. Let the pie cool completely before serving to allow the filling to set.

Rabbit stew

Ingredients:

- 1 lb rabbit meat
- 2 cups chicken broth
- 1 onion, diced
- 2 carrots, sliced
- 1 potato, diced
- 1 tbsp olive oil
- Salt and pepper to taste

Equipment:

1. Knife
2. Cutting board
3. Pot
4. Ladle
5. Skillet
6. Wooden spoon

Methods:

Step 1: Start by cutting the rabbit into small pieces.
Step 2: In a large pot, heat some oil over medium heat.
Step 3: Add the rabbit pieces to the pot and brown them on all sides.
Step 4: Add chopped onions, carrots, and celery to the pot.
Step 5: Pour in some chicken or vegetable broth to cover the rabbit pieces.
Step 6: Season with salt, pepper, and herbs like thyme and rosemary.
Step 7: Cover the pot and let the stew simmer for about 1-2 hours.
Step 8: Serve the rabbit stew hot with crusty bread or over mashed potatoes. Enjoy!

Helpful Tips:

1. Start by browning the rabbit pieces in a large pot for added flavor.
2. Add aromatics like onions, carrots, and garlic to enhance the overall taste of the stew.
3. Use a combination of broth and red wine for a rich and flavorful liquid base.
4. Consider adding fresh herbs like thyme, rosemary, and bay leaves for added depth of flavor.
5. Cook the stew low and slow to ensure the rabbit meat becomes tender and falls off the bone.
6. Taste and adjust seasonings as needed, adding salt and pepper to taste.
7. Serve the rabbit stew with crusty bread or over mashed potatoes for a hearty meal.

Indian pudding (cornmeal pudding)

Ingredients:

- 1 cup cornmeal
- 4 cups water
- 1 cup milk
- 1/2 cup sugar
- 1/2 tsp cardamom powder
- 1/4 cup chopped nuts

Equipment:

1. Mixing bowl
2. Whisk
3. Saucepan
4. Wooden spoon
5. Sieve
6. Ramekins

Methods:

Step 1: In a saucepan, bring 3 cups of milk to a boil over medium heat.
Step 2: Slowly whisk in 1/2 cup of cornmeal and reduce heat to low.
Step 3: Cook for 10-15 minutes, stirring constantly until the mixture thickens.
Step 4: Add 1/2 cup of sugar, 1/4 cup of butter, and a pinch of salt, stirring until well combined.
Step 5: In a separate bowl, beat 2 eggs and then slowly whisk in a small amount of the hot cornmeal mixture.
Step 6: Gradually pour the egg mixture back into the saucepan, stirring constantly.
Step 7: Cook for an additional 2-3 minutes until the pudding is thick and

creamy.
Step 8: Remove from heat and stir in 1 teaspoon of vanilla extract.
Step 9: Let the pudding cool slightly before serving. Enjoy your Indian pudding!

Helpful Tips:

1. Use a heavy-bottomed saucepan to prevent burning.
2. Stir constantly while adding the cornmeal to prevent clumping.
3. Add sugar slowly while stirring to ensure smooth incorporation.
4. Use whole milk for a rich and creamy pudding.
5. Add spices like cinnamon, cardamom, or nutmeg for a warm flavor.
6. Cook pudding on low heat to prevent scorching.
7. Allow pudding to cool slightly before serving for a firmer texture.
8. Top with nuts, raisins, or a dollop of whipped cream for added flavor and texture.
9. Refrigerate leftovers and reheat gently on the stovetop or in the microwave.
10. Enjoy your homemade Indian pudding!

Acorn bread

Ingredients:

- 2 cups acorn flour
- 1/2 cup sugar
- 1 tsp baking soda
- 1/2 tsp salt
- 2 eggs
- 1 cup milk
- 1/4 cup butter

Equipment:

1. Mixing bowl
2. Whisk
3. Measuring cups and spoons
4. Baking pan
5. Oven mitts

Methods:

Step 1: Preheat your oven to 350°F (175°C) and grease a loaf pan.
Step 2: In a large mixing bowl, combine 2 cups of acorn flour, 1 cup of all-purpose flour, 1 tsp of baking soda, and a pinch of salt.
Step 3: In a separate bowl, whisk together 2 eggs, 1/2 cup of honey, and 1/4 cup of melted butter.
Step 4: Gradually stir the wet ingredients into the dry ingredients until well combined.
Step 5: Pour the batter into the loaf pan and bake for 45-50 minutes, or until a toothpick inserted into the center comes out clean.
Step 6: Allow the bread to cool before slicing and serving. Enjoy your homemade acorn bread!

Helpful Tips:

1. Preheat your oven to 350 degrees Fahrenheit before starting to make acorn bread.
2. Grind the acorn nuts into a fine meal using a food processor or mortar and pestle.
3. Sift the acorn meal with all-purpose flour to create a lighter texture in the bread.
4. Use a combination of honey and sugar as sweeteners for a more complex flavor profile.
5. Add a touch of cinnamon or nutmeg for a warm and cozy taste.
6. Mix in chopped nuts or dried fruits for added texture and flavor.
7. Bake the acorn bread in a greased loaf pan for about 45-50 minutes or until a toothpick inserted in the center comes out clean.
8. Allow the bread to cool before slicing and serving. Enjoy!

Smoked trout

Ingredients:

- 400g smoked trout
- 1 lemon
- 2 tbsp olive oil
- Fresh dill

Equipment:

1. Chef's knife
2. Cutting board
3. Mixing bowls
4. Skillet
5. Tongs

Methods:

Step 1: Preheat the smoker to 225°F and prepare the wood chips.
Step 2: Rinse the trout under cold water and pat dry with paper towels.
Step 3: Season the trout with salt, pepper, and your choice of herbs or spices.
Step 4: Place the trout on the smoker racks skin-side down.
Step 5: Smoke the trout for 1-2 hours, or until it reaches an internal temperature of 145°F.
Step 6: Remove the trout from the smoker and let it rest for a few minutes before serving.
Step 7: Enjoy your delicious smoked trout!

Helpful Tips:

1. Start by preparing your smoked trout by removing the skin and any bones.
2. Consider incorporating the smoked trout into dishes like salads, pasta, or on top of crackers or bread.
3. Experiment with pairing the smoked trout with ingredients like dill, lemon, capers, or cream cheese for added flavor.
4. Be cautious not to overcook the smoked trout, as it can become dry and lose its delicate flavor.
5. Store any leftover smoked trout in an airtight container in the refrigerator for up to 3 days.
6. Enjoy the unique and smoky flavor of the trout in a variety of dishes!

Sunchoke soup

Ingredients:

- 1 pound sunchokes
- 1 onion
- 2 cloves garlic
- 4 cups vegetable broth
- 1/2 cup heavy cream
- Salt and pepper to taste

Equipment:

1. Knife
2. Cutting board
3. Pot
4. Immersion blender
5. Ladle

Methods:

Step 1: Peel and chop 1 pound of sunchokes into small pieces.
Step 2: Heat 2 tablespoons of olive oil in a large pot over medium heat.
Step 3: Add 1 chopped onion and 2 minced garlic cloves to the pot and cook until softened.
Step 4: Add the chopped sunchokes to the pot and cook for 5 minutes.
Step 5: Pour in 4 cups of vegetable broth and bring to a simmer.
Step 6: Cover the pot and let the soup cook for 20-25 minutes, until the sunchokes are tender.
Step 7: Blend the soup until smooth using an immersion blender.
Step 8: Season with salt and pepper to taste before serving hot.

Helpful Tips:

1. Start by washing and peeling the sunchokes to remove dirt and tough outer skin.
2. Dice the sunchokes into uniform pieces to ensure even cooking.
3. In a large pot, sauté onions and garlic in olive oil until translucent and fragrant.
4. Add the diced sunchokes and vegetable broth to the pot, bringing it to a boil.
5. Reduce heat and let the soup simmer until the sunchokes are tender, about 20-25 minutes.
6. Use an immersion blender to puree the soup until smooth.
7. Season with salt, pepper, and herbs to taste.
8. Add a splash of cream or coconut milk for added creaminess.
9. Garnish with fresh herbs or toasted nuts before serving. Enjoy your delicious Sunchoke soup!

Maple sugar candy

Ingredients:

- 2 cups of maple syrup
- 1/2 teaspoon of vanilla extract
- 1/4 teaspoon of salt
- 1/2 cup of chopped nuts (optional)

Equipment:

1. Mixing bowl
2. Saucepan
3. Whisk
4. Candy thermometer
5. Wooden spoon

Methods:

Step 1: In a medium saucepan, combine 2 cups of pure maple syrup.
Step 2: Bring the maple syrup to a boil over medium heat, stirring constantly.
Step 3: Continue to cook the syrup, without stirring, until it reaches 235°F on a candy thermometer.
Step 4: Remove the saucepan from heat and let the bubbles subside.
Step 5: Beat the mixture with a wooden spoon until it thickens and becomes creamy.
Step 6: Quickly pour the mixture onto a parchment-lined baking sheet.
Step 7: Let the mixture cool and harden, then break it into pieces to enjoy your homemade maple sugar candy.

Helpful Tips:

1. Use real maple syrup for the best flavor.
2. Make sure to use a candy thermometer to achieve the correct temperature (235°F) for the candy to set properly.
3. Stir constantly to prevent burning and ensure even heating.
4. Brush the sides of the pan with water to prevent crystallization.
5. Once the mixture reaches 235°F, remove from heat and let it cool slightly before pouring into molds.
6. Allow the candy to set at room temperature for several hours before removing from molds.
7. Store in an airtight container to prevent drying out.

Bear stew

Ingredients:

- 2 lbs bear meat
- 2 onions
- 4 carrots
- 4 potatoes
- 4 cups beef broth
- Salt and pepper
- 2 garlic cloves

Equipment:

1. Knife
2. Cutting board
3. Pot
4. Ladle
5. Skillet

Methods:

Step 1: Start by cutting up pieces of bear meat into bite-sized chunks.
Step 2: Season the meat with salt and pepper.
Step 3: In a large pot, heat oil over medium heat and brown the meat on all sides.
Step 4: Add diced onions, carrots, and celery to the pot and cook until they are softened.
Step 5: Pour in beef broth and bring the stew to a simmer.
Step 6: Add in chopped potatoes, mushrooms, and a bay leaf for flavor.
Step 7: Cover and let the stew simmer for 2-3 hours until the meat is tender.
Step 8: Serve hot and enjoy your hearty bear stew!

Helpful Tips:

1. Use a tough cut of bear meat, like the shoulder, for stew as it will become tender when slow cooked.
2. Marinate the bear meat in vinegar or buttermilk for several hours to help remove any gamey flavor.
3. Sear the bear meat in a hot pan before adding it to the stew to enhance the flavor.
4. Add plenty of aromatics like onions, garlic, and herbs to the stew for added depth of flavor.
5. Use a rich broth or stock as the base of the stew to enhance the overall taste.
6. Cook the stew low and slow for at least 3-4 hours to ensure the meat is tender and flavorful.

Wild mushroom risotto

Ingredients:

- 1 cup Arborio rice
- 4 cups chicken or vegetable broth
- 1/2 cup white wine
- 1 cup mixed wild mushrooms
- 1/2 cup grated Parmesan cheese
- 1 shallot, finely chopped
- 2 garlic cloves, minced
- Salt and pepper to taste

Equipment:

1. Chef's knife
2. Cutting board
3. Wooden spoon
4. Deep saucepan
5. Ladle

Methods:

Step 1: Heat 1 tablespoon of olive oil in a large pan over medium heat.
Step 2: Add 1 finely chopped onion and sauté for 5 minutes until translucent.
Step 3: Add 2 cups of Arborio rice and cook for 2 minutes, stirring constantly.
Step 4: Pour in 1/2 cup of dry white wine and stir until absorbed.
Step 5: Slowly add 6 cups of warm vegetable broth, 1 cup at a time, stirring frequently until each cup is absorbed.
Step 6: Stir in 1 cup of mixed wild mushrooms and cook for 5 minutes.
Step 7: Remove from heat and stir in 1/2 cup of grated Parmesan cheese.
Step 8: Season with salt and pepper, then serve hot.

Helpful Tips:

1. Use a variety of wild mushrooms for depth of flavor, such as porcini, chanterelle, and shiitake.
2. Sweat onions and garlic in butter before adding Arborio rice to develop flavor.
3. Deglaze the pan with white wine before adding chicken or vegetable stock, one ladle at a time, stirring constantly until absorbed.
4. Add fresh thyme and a splash of cream for richness.
5. Finish with grated Parmesan cheese and a drizzle of truffle oil before serving.
6. Garnish with chopped parsley and more Parmesan for a delicious and elegant presentation.

Cranberry sauce

Ingredients:

- 1 cup fresh cranberries
- 1/2 cup orange juice
- 1/2 cup sugar
- 1/4 cup water

Equipment:

1. Mixing bowl
2. Whisk
3. Saucepan
4. Wooden spoon
5. Ladle

Methods:

Step 1: Combine 1 cup of sugar and 1 cup of water in a saucepan over medium heat.
Step 2: Stir until the sugar dissolves completely.
Step 3: Add 12 ounces of fresh cranberries to the saucepan.
Step 4: Bring the mixture to a boil.
Step 5: Reduce the heat and let the cranberries simmer for about 10 minutes.
Step 6: Stir occasionally until the cranberries burst.
Step 7: Remove from heat and let the sauce cool.
Step 8: Store in the refrigerator until ready to serve.
Step 9: Enjoy your homemade cranberry sauce with your favorite dishes!

Helpful Tips:

1. Start by combining fresh cranberries, sugar, water, and any desired spices in a saucepan.
2. Bring the mixture to a boil, then reduce heat and simmer until the cranberries burst and the sauce thickens.
3. Stir occasionally to prevent sticking and burning.
4. Taste the sauce and adjust the sweetness or acidity as needed with more sugar or lemon juice.
5. For added flavor, try incorporating orange zest, cinnamon, cloves, or ginger.
6. Let the sauce cool before serving to allow the flavors to meld.
7. Store any leftovers in an airtight container in the refrigerator for up to two weeks.
8. Enjoy your homemade cranberry sauce with turkey, roast chicken, or as a topping for desserts.

Rabbit fry

Ingredients:

- 1 rabbit (cut into pieces)
- 2 tablespoons of oil
- 1 onion (chopped)
- 2 cloves of garlic (minced)
- Salt and pepper to taste
- 1 teaspoon of paprika
- 1/2 cup of chicken broth

Equipment:

1. Frying pan
2. Saucepan
3. Baking sheet
4. Mixing bowl
5. Whisk

Methods:

Step 1: Cut the rabbit meat into small pieces.
Step 2: Marinate the meat with salt, pepper, and any other desired spices.
Step 3: Heat oil in a pan over medium heat.
Step 4: Add the marinated rabbit pieces into the pan.
Step 5: Fry the meat until it is browned on all sides.
Step 6: Add chopped onions, garlic, and herbs to the pan.
Step 7: Cook until the onions are translucent.
Step 8: Add tomato sauce or broth to the pan.
Step 9: Let the meat simmer in the sauce for 15-20 minutes.
Step 10: Serve hot with rice or bread. Enjoy your delicious rabbit fry!

Helpful Tips:

1. Start by marinating the rabbit pieces with a mixture of garlic, ginger, salt, pepper, and a splash of vinegar for at least an hour.
2. Dredge the marinated rabbit pieces in a mixture of flour, cornstarch, salt, and pepper before frying to give them a crispy coating.
3. Use a deep fryer or a large skillet with enough oil to fully submerge the rabbit pieces for even cooking.
4. Fry the rabbit pieces in batches to avoid overcrowding and ensure they cook evenly.
5. Cook the rabbit pieces for about 6-8 minutes, turning occasionally, until golden brown and cooked through.
6. Serve the rabbit fry hot with your favorite dipping sauce or side dishes. Enjoy!

Deer jerky

Ingredients:

- 1 lb of deer meat
- 1/4 cup soy sauce
- 2 tbsp Worcestershire sauce
- 1 tsp garlic powder
- 1 tsp onion powder
- 1/2 tsp black pepper

Equipment:

1. Chef's knife
2. Cutting board
3. Mixing bowl
4. Skillet
5. Tongs

Methods:

Step 1: Slice the deer meat into thin strips, cutting against the grain for a tender jerky.
Step 2: Marinate the meat strips in a mixture of soy sauce, Worcestershire sauce, brown sugar, garlic powder, and black pepper for at least 4 hours.
Step 3: Preheat the oven to 175°F (80°C) and line a baking sheet with foil.
Step 4: Arrange the marinated meat strips on the baking sheet, making sure they don't overlap.
Step 5: Bake the jerky in the oven for 3-4 hours, flipping the strips halfway through.
Step 6: Let the jerky cool before enjoying this delicious snack.

Helpful Tips:

1. Start by selecting lean cuts of venison, such as the hindquarters or backstrap, for the best jerky.
2. Freeze the meat for a few hours to make it easier to slice thinly against the grain.
3. Marinate the sliced meat in a mixture of soy sauce, Worcestershire sauce, liquid smoke, and your favorite seasonings for at least 4 hours or overnight.
4. Pat the meat dry before placing it on a dehydrator tray or baking sheet.
5. Dry the jerky at 160°F for 4-6 hours, or until it reaches your desired level of chewiness.
6. Store the jerky in an airtight container to maintain freshness. Enjoy as a protein-packed snack!

Cornbread stuffing

Ingredients:

- Cornbread (6 cups)
- Chicken broth (1 1/2 cups)
- Celery (3 stalks, chopped)
- Onion (1, diced)
- Sage (1 tsp)
- Butter (1/4 cup)
- Salt and Pepper to taste

Equipment:

1. Mixing bowl
2. Whisk
3. Baking dish
4. Kitchen knife
5. Cutting board
6. Saucepan

Methods:

Step 1: Preheat the oven to 350°F and grease a baking dish.
Step 2: In a large skillet, cook diced onion and celery in butter until softened.
Step 3: In a large mixing bowl, combine cornbread cubes, cooked vegetables, broth, beaten eggs, and seasonings.
Step 4: Mix until well combined, then pour into the prepared baking dish.
Step 5: Cover with foil and bake for 30 minutes.
Step 6: Remove foil and bake for an additional 15 minutes or until golden brown on top.
Step 7: Let cool slightly before serving. Enjoy your delicious cornbread stuffing!

Helpful Tips:

1. Start by preparing your cornbread a day in advance to allow it to dry out slightly.
2. Use a mix of cornbread and white bread for added texture and flavor.
3. Sauté onions, celery, and garlic in butter for a savory base.
4. Add in herbs such as sage, thyme, and rosemary for traditional stuffing flavors.
5. Mix in chicken or vegetable broth to keep the stuffing moist.
6. Consider adding in cooked sausage or bacon for extra protein and flavor.
7. For a vegetarian option, use mushrooms or roasted vegetables instead.
8. Bake the stuffing until golden and crispy on top before serving.

Juniper berry roasted quail

Ingredients:

- 4 quails
- 1 tbsp juniper berries
- 2 tbsp olive oil
- Salt and pepper
- Fresh herbs

Equipment:

1. Knife
2. Cutting board
3. Skillet
4. Roasting pan
5. Tongs

Methods:

Step 1: Preheat the oven to 400°F.
Step 2: Rinse the quails in cold water and pat dry with paper towels.
Step 3: In a small bowl, combine crushed juniper berries, salt, pepper, and olive oil to make a paste.
Step 4: Rub the juniper berry paste all over the quails, making sure to coat them evenly.
Step 5: Place the quails in a roasting pan and roast in the preheated oven for 20-25 minutes, or until the internal temperature reaches 165°F.
Step 6: Remove the quails from the oven and let them rest for 5 minutes before serving.
Step 7: Enjoy your delicious juniper berry roasted quail!

Helpful Tips:

1. Start by rinsing and drying the quail thoroughly before seasoning.
2. Use a mortar and pestle to crush the juniper berries before mixing with salt, pepper, and herbs for a rub.
3. Gently massage the juniper berry rub onto the quail, making sure to evenly coat the skin.
4. Preheat your oven to a high temperature for a quick roast, around 450°F.
5. Place the quail in a roasting pan and cook for about 20-25 minutes until the skin is crispy and the meat is cooked through.
6. Let the quail rest for a few minutes before serving to allow the juices to redistribute.
7. Enjoy your delicious and flavorful juniper berry roasted quail!

Sweet potato casserole

Ingredients:

- 2 large sweet potatoes
- 1/2 cup brown sugar
- 1/4 cup butter
- 1 tsp cinnamon
- 1/2 cup chopped pecans

Equipment:

1. Mixing bowl
2. Potato masher
3. Baking dish
4. Whisk
5. Measuring cups
6. Oven mitts

Methods:

Step 1: Preheat the oven to 350°F.
Step 2: Peel and dice 3-4 sweet potatoes.
Step 3: Boil the sweet potatoes in water until tender, then mash them.
Step 4: Mix the mashed sweet potatoes with 1/2 cup of brown sugar, 1/4 cup of melted butter, 1 tsp of cinnamon, and a pinch of salt.
Step 5: Spread the sweet potato mixture in a baking dish.
Step 6: In a separate bowl, mix 1/2 cup of brown sugar, 1/4 cup of flour, 1/4 cup of melted butter, and 1 cup of chopped pecans.
Step 7: Sprinkle the pecan mixture over the sweet potatoes.
Step 8: Bake for 30 minutes, or until golden brown.

Helpful Tips:

1. Use fresh sweet potatoes for the best texture and flavor.
2. Peel and chop the sweet potatoes into uniform pieces for even cooking.
3. Boil the sweet potatoes until they are fork-tender before mashing.
4. Add brown sugar, cinnamon, and nutmeg for a classic sweet potato casserole flavor.
5. Mix in butter and cream to make the casserole creamy and rich.
6. Top the casserole with a crunchy pecan streusel for added texture.
7. Bake the casserole until it is bubbly and golden brown on top.
8. Let the casserole cool for a few minutes before serving to let the flavors meld together.

Elk burgers

Ingredients:

- 1 lb ground elk meat
- 1/4 cup breadcrumbs
- 1/4 cup diced onion
- 1/2 tsp salt
- 1/4 tsp pepper
- 4 hamburger buns

Equipment:

1. Knife
2. Cutting board
3. Skillet
4. Spatula
5. Tongs

Methods:

Step 1: Start by mixing ground elk meat with your desired seasonings and spices in a large bowl.
Step 2: Form the seasoned meat into patties, ensuring they are evenly shaped and seasoned.
Step 3: Preheat a skillet or grill over medium-high heat.
Step 4: Place the elk patties on the skillet or grill and cook for about 4-5 minutes on each side, or until they reach your desired level of doneness.
Step 5: Once cooked, remove the elk burgers from the heat and let them rest for a few minutes.
Step 6: Serve the elk burgers on buns with your favorite toppings and enjoy!

Helpful Tips:

1. Start with high-quality elk meat, preferably grass-fed and pasture-raised.
2. Season the elk burgers with salt, pepper, and your choice of herbs or spices.
3. Form the elk burger patties with a light touch to prevent overworking the meat.
4. Cook the elk burgers on a hot grill or skillet for a few minutes on each side until they reach an internal temperature of 160°F.
5. Avoid pressing down on the burgers while cooking to retain juices.
6. Serve the elk burgers on a toasted bun with your favorite toppings and condiments.
7. Enjoy with a side of fresh salad or roasted vegetables for a complete meal.

Succotash (corn and lima beans)

Ingredients:

- 2 cups of corn
- 1 cup of lima beans
- 1/4 cup of butter
- 1/2 teaspoon of salt

Equipment:

1. Knife
2. Cutting board
3. Skillet
4. Saucepan
5. Wooden spoon

Methods:

Step 1: Heat oil in a large skillet over medium heat.
Step 2: Add diced onions and cook until translucent.
Step 3: Stir in chopped bell peppers and cook for a few more minutes.
Step 4: Add corn kernels and lima beans to the skillet.
Step 5: Season with salt, pepper, and your favorite herbs.
Step 6: Cook for about 10-15 minutes, stirring occasionally.
Step 7: Taste and adjust seasoning if needed.
Step 8: Serve the succotash hot as a side dish or as a main course.
Step 9: Enjoy your delicious and nutritious corn and lima bean succotash!

Helpful Tips:

1. Start by blanching fresh lima beans for a few minutes in boiling water before adding to the dish.

2. Choose sweet, fresh corn for the best flavor in your succotash.
3. Sauté diced onions and bell peppers in butter until soft before adding the corn and lima beans.
4. Add a splash of chicken or vegetable broth to the succotash for extra flavor and moisture.
5. Season with salt, pepper, and garlic powder to taste.
6. Top with fresh herbs like parsley or thyme before serving.
7. Serve as a side dish or even as a main course with grilled protein.

Blueberry muffins

Ingredients:

- 1 cup of blueberries
- 1 and 1/2 cups of flour
- 1/2 cup of sugar
- 2 teaspoons of baking powder
- 1/2 cup of milk
- 1/4 cup of vegetable oil
- 1 egg

Equipment:

1. Mixing bowl
2. Measuring cups and spoons
3. Whisk
4. Muffin tin
5. Spatula

Methods:

Step 1: Preheat the oven to 375°F and grease a muffin tin.
Step 2: In a large bowl, mix together 2 cups of flour, 2/3 cup of sugar, 2 teaspoons of baking powder, and a pinch of salt.
Step 3: In a separate bowl, whisk together 1 egg, 1 cup of milk, and 1/4 cup of melted butter.
Step 4: Gently fold the wet ingredients into the dry ingredients until just combined.
Step 5: Gently fold in 1 cup of fresh blueberries.
Step 6: Spoon the batter into the muffin tin, filling each cup about 2/3 full.
Step 7: Bake for 20-25 minutes, or until a toothpick inserted into the center of a muffin comes out clean.

Step 8: Allow the muffins to cool before serving. Enjoy your delicious blueberry muffins!

Helpful Tips:

1. Start by preheating your oven to the correct temperature as stated in the recipe (usually around 375°F).
2. Make sure to properly measure all ingredients for accurate results.
3. Combine dry ingredients (flour, sugar, baking powder, salt) in one bowl and wet ingredients (eggs, milk, oil) in another.
4. Gently fold the wet ingredients into the dry ingredients until just combined to avoid overmixing.
5. Carefully fold in the blueberries to prevent them from breaking.
6. Fill muffin cups about 2/3 full to allow room for rising.
7. Bake for the recommended time, checking for doneness with a toothpick before removing from oven.
8. Let cool before enjoying your delicious blueberry muffins.

Bison meatloaf

Ingredients:

- 1 lb ground bison
- 1/2 cup breadcrumbs
- 1/4 cup diced onions
- 1/4 cup diced bell peppers
- 1/4 cup ketchup
- 1 egg
- Salt and pepper to taste

Equipment:

1. Mixing bowl
2. Whisk
3. Mixing spoon
4. Baking dish
5. Measuring cups
6. Oven mitts

Methods:

Step 1: Preheat the oven to 350 degrees Fahrenheit.
Step 2: In a large bowl, combine 1 pound of ground bison meat, 1/2 cup of breadcrumbs, 1/4 cup of finely chopped onion, 1/4 cup of ketchup, 1 egg, and salt and pepper to taste.
Step 3: Mix the ingredients together until well combined.
Step 4: Form the mixture into a loaf shape and place it in a baking dish.
Step 5: Spread additional ketchup on top of the meatloaf.
Step 6: Bake in the preheated oven for 45-50 minutes, or until the meatloaf is cooked through.
Step 7: Let the meatloaf rest for 5 minutes before slicing and serving. Enjoy your delicious bison meatloaf!

Helpful Tips:

1. Start with high-quality ground bison meat for the best flavor.
2. Mix in your favorite seasonings, such as garlic, onion, dried herbs, and Worcestershire sauce, to enhance the natural flavor of the bison.
3. Add breadcrumbs or oatmeal to help bind the meatloaf together.
4. Consider adding finely chopped vegetables, like carrots or bell peppers, for added texture and nutrition.
5. Bake the meatloaf at a lower temperature (around 350°F) to prevent it from drying out.
6. Let the meatloaf rest for a few minutes before slicing to allow the juices to redistribute. Serve with a flavorful gravy or sauce on the side.

Purslane salad

Ingredients:

- 4 cups purslane
- 1 cucumber, sliced
- 1 red onion, thinly sliced
- 1 cup cherry tomatoes, halved
- 1/4 cup feta cheese
- 2 tbsp olive oil
- 2 tbsp lemon juice

Equipment:

1. Knife
2. Cutting board
3. Mixing bowl
4. Salad spinner
5. Salad tongs

Methods:

Step 1: Rinse 2 cups of purslane thoroughly under cold water.
Step 2: Pat the purslane dry with a clean kitchen towel or paper towels.
Step 3: Chop the purslane into bite-sized pieces and place in a large mixing bowl.
Step 4: Add diced tomatoes, cucumbers, and red onions to the bowl.
Step 5: In a small bowl, whisk together olive oil, lemon juice, salt, and pepper to make a dressing.
Step 6: Pour the dressing over the salad and toss to combine.
Step 7: Refrigerate the salad for at least 30 minutes before serving.
Step 8: Enjoy your refreshing and nutritious purslane salad!

Helpful Tips:

1. Start by washing the purslane thoroughly to remove any dirt or debris.
2. Remove any tough stems and separate the leaves for the salad.
3. Mix the purslane with other fresh ingredients like tomatoes, cucumbers, and herbs.
4. Add a light vinaigrette dressing with olive oil, lemon juice, salt, and pepper.
5. For added flavor, try incorporating some crumbled feta cheese or toasted nuts.
6. Serve the purslane salad chilled to enhance its crisp texture and refreshing taste.
7. Experiment with different combinations of ingredients to find your perfect balance of flavors.

Salmon cakes

Ingredients:

- 1 lb cooked salmon
- 1/2 cup bread crumbs
- 1/4 cup chopped onion
- 2 tbsp mayonnaise
- 1 egg
- Salt and pepper
- Lemon wedges, for serving

Equipment:

1. Mixing bowl
2. Whisk
3. Skillet
4. Spatula
5. Knife

Methods:

Step 1: In a bowl, mix together cooked salmon, breadcrumbs, chopped onion, parsley, and a beaten egg.
Step 2: Form the mixture into patties and coat with flour.
Step 3: Heat oil in a skillet over medium heat.
Step 4: Place the salmon cakes in the skillet and cook for 4-5 minutes on each side, until golden brown.
Step 5: Serve hot with your favorite dipping sauce or a squeeze of lemon juice. Enjoy your delicious salmon cakes!

Helpful Tips:

1. Start by choosing fresh salmon fillets for the best flavor.
2. Cook the salmon fillets by baking or grilling them until they are just cooked through.
3. Let the salmon cool before flaking it into small pieces.
4. Mix the flaked salmon with breadcrumbs, finely diced onions, mayonnaise, mustard, and seasonings.
5. Form the mixture into patties and chill them in the refrigerator for at least 30 minutes.
6. Heat oil in a skillet and cook the salmon cakes until they are golden brown on both sides.
7. Serve the salmon cakes with a side of lemon wedges and a fresh salad for a delicious meal.

Elk stew

Ingredients:

- 2 lbs of elk meat
- 1 onion, diced
- 4 carrots, chopped
- 4 potatoes, cubed
- 2 cups of beef broth
- 1 tsp of salt
- 1/2 tsp of pepper
- 1 tsp of thyme

Equipment:

1. Pot
2. Wooden spoon
3. Chef's knife
4. Cutting board
5. Ladle

Methods:

Step 1: Start by seasoning the elk meat with salt, pepper, and any other desired seasonings.
Step 2: Heat oil in a large pot over medium heat and brown the elk meat on all sides.
Step 3: Add chopped onions, celery, carrots, and garlic to the pot and sauté until the vegetables are tender.
Step 4: Pour in beef broth and red wine, then bring to a simmer.
Step 5: Add in diced tomatoes, potatoes, and any other desired vegetables.
Step 6: Cover the pot and let the stew simmer for at least 2 hours, stirring occasionally.
Step 7: Serve hot and enjoy your delicious elk stew.

Helpful Tips:

1. Marinate the elk meat overnight in a mixture of red wine, garlic, and herbs for added flavor.
2. Brown the meat in a hot skillet before adding it to the stew to seal in the juices.
3. Use a combination of onions, carrots, celery, and potatoes for a well-balanced stew.
4. Add in fresh herbs like thyme and rosemary for a fragrant aroma.
5. Consider adding a splash of Worcestershire sauce or balsamic vinegar for a tangy kick.
6. Simmer the stew on low heat for several hours to allow the flavors to meld together.

Pumpkin soup

Ingredients:

- 1 small pumpkin (500g), peeled and chopped
- 1 onion, diced
- 2 cloves of garlic, minced
- 4 cups of vegetable broth
- 1 tsp of ground cinnamon
- 1/2 tsp of nutmeg
- Salt and pepper to taste

Equipment:

1. Knife
2. Cutting board
3. Pot
4. Blender
5. Ladle

Methods:

Step 1: Preheat your oven to 400°F.
Step 2: Cut a medium-sized pumpkin in half and remove the seeds with a spoon.
Step 3: Place the pumpkin halves on a baking sheet and roast in the oven for 45 minutes, or until tender.
Step 4: Scoop out the flesh of the pumpkin and place it in a blender.
Step 5: Add vegetable broth, garlic, onion, and your choice of spices.
Step 6: Blend until smooth.
Step 7: Pour the mixture into a pot and simmer on low heat for 15 minutes.
Step 8: Serve hot and enjoy your delicious pumpkin soup!

Helpful Tips:

1. Start by roasting the pumpkin in the oven to enhance its flavor.
2. Use a combination of spices like cinnamon, nutmeg, and ginger to add warmth to the soup.
3. Saute onions and garlic in a large pot before adding in the roasted pumpkin.
4. Add vegetable or chicken broth to the pot and let the soup simmer for at least 20 minutes.
5. Blend the soup with an immersion blender until smooth.
6. Finish the soup with a swirl of heavy cream or coconut milk for added richness.
7. Serve with toasted pumpkin seeds or a sprinkle of fresh herbs for garnish.

Maple glazed carrots

Ingredients:

- 1 lb of carrots
- 2 tbsp of maple syrup
- 1 tbsp of butter
- Salt and pepper to taste

Equipment:

1. Mixing bowl
2. Saucepan
3. Wooden spoon
4. Basting brush
5. Chef's knife

Methods:

Step 1: Peel and slice carrots into desired size.
Step 2: In a saucepan, combine butter, maple syrup, and a pinch of salt.
Step 3: Add carrots to the saucepan and coat them in the mixture.
Step 4: Cook on medium heat, stirring occasionally, until the carrots are tender (about 10-15 minutes).
Step 5: Once the carrots are cooked, remove them from the heat.
Step 6: Serve the maple glazed carrots as a delicious side dish to complement your meal. Enjoy!

Helpful Tips:

1. Start by peeling and slicing the carrots into even, bite-sized pieces.
2. In a saucepan, combine maple syrup, butter, and a pinch of salt over medium heat.

3. Add the carrots to the saucepan and toss to evenly coat in the maple glaze.
4. Simmer the carrots in the glaze for about 10-15 minutes, stirring occasionally.
5. Test the carrots with a fork to ensure they are cooked to your desired level of tenderness.
6. Serve the maple glazed carrots hot as a delicious and sweet side dish.
7. Garnish with fresh herbs or nuts for added flavor and texture.

Wild rice salad

Ingredients:

- 1 cup wild rice
- 1 red bell pepper, diced
- 1/2 cup dried cranberries
- 1/4 cup sliced almonds
- 2 tbsp olive oil
- 2 tbsp balsamic vinegar

Equipment:

1. Mixing bowl
2. Whisk
3. Knife
4. Cutting board
5. Saucepan

Methods:

Step 1: Rinse 1 cup of wild rice in a fine-mesh strainer under cold water.
Step 2: Place the rinsed rice in a pot with 4 cups of water and bring to a boil.
Step 3: Reduce heat, cover, and simmer for 45-55 minutes, until the rice is tender.
Step 4: Drain any excess water and let the rice cool completely.
Step 5: In a large bowl, combine the cooled rice with chopped vegetables like bell pepper, cucumber, and cherry tomatoes.
Step 6: Add in chopped herbs like parsley and mint.
Step 7: Drizzle with a simple dressing of olive oil, lemon juice, salt, and pepper.
Step 8: Toss everything together until well combined and serve chilled. Enjoy your wild rice salad!

Helpful Tips:

1. Rinse the wild rice thoroughly to remove any excess starch.
2. Cook the wild rice in broth instead of water for added flavor.
3. Add a mix of colorful vegetables like bell peppers, cherry tomatoes, and cucumbers for a visually appealing dish.
4. Incorporate fresh herbs like dill, parsley, or basil for an extra burst of flavor.
5. Try adding toasted nuts or seeds for added crunch and texture.
6. Make a simple vinaigrette dressing using olive oil, vinegar, and a touch of honey for a sweet and tangy flavor.
7. Chill the salad for at least an hour before serving to allow the flavors to meld together.

Sunflower seed bread

Ingredients:

- 2 cups whole wheat flour
- 1 cup sunflower seeds
- 1/4 cup honey
- 1 tbsp yeast
- 1 tsp salt
- 1 1/4 cup warm water

Equipment:

1. Mixing bowl
2. Whisk
3. Bread pan
4. Measuring cup
5. Spoon
6. Oven

Methods:

Step 1: In a mixing bowl, combine 1 cup of warm water and 2 tablespoons of honey. Stir until honey is dissolved.
Step 2: Add 1 packet of active dry yeast and let it sit for 5 minutes until it becomes frothy.
Step 3: Mix in 2 cups of bread flour, 1 cup of whole wheat flour, 1/2 cup of sunflower seeds, and 1 teaspoon of salt.
Step 4: Knead the dough for 10 minutes until it becomes smooth.
Step 5: Place dough in a greased bowl, cover with a towel, and let it rise for 1 hour.
Step 6: Shape dough into a loaf, brush with egg wash, sprinkle with sunflower seeds, and bake at 375°F for 30-35 minutes.

Helpful Tips:

1. Start by gathering all of your ingredients: sunflower seeds, flour, yeast, honey, salt, and water.
2. Toast the sunflower seeds in a dry skillet over medium heat until they are lightly browned and fragrant.
3. Combine the flour, yeast, honey, salt, water, and toasted sunflower seeds in a mixing bowl.
4. Knead the dough until smooth and elastic, then let it rise in a warm place until doubled in size.
5. Shape the dough into a loaf and place it in a greased bread pan.
6. Bake the bread in a preheated oven until it is golden brown and sounds hollow when tapped on the bottom.
7. Let the bread cool before slicing and enjoying!

Buffalo burgers

Ingredients:

- 1 lb ground buffalo meat
- 1/4 cup bread crumbs
- 1/4 cup BBQ sauce
- 1/2 tsp garlic powder
- Salt and pepper to taste

Equipment:

1. Skillet
2. Spatula
3. Tongs
4. Chef's knife
5. Cutting board
6. Grill pan

Methods:

Step 1: Start by seasoning ground buffalo meat with salt, pepper, and any desired spices.
Step 2: Form the seasoned meat into burger patties, making sure they are evenly shaped and sized.
Step 3: Preheat a grill or skillet to medium-high heat.
Step 4: Cook the buffalo burgers for 4-5 minutes on each side, or until they reach an internal temperature of 160°F.
Step 5: Add cheese slices to the burgers during the last minute of cooking, if desired.
Step 6: Toast burger buns on the grill for a couple of minutes.
Step 7: Assemble the burgers with toppings like lettuce, tomato, and onion. Enjoy your delicious buffalo burgers!

Helpful Tips:

1. Make sure to season the buffalo meat well to enhance its flavor.
2. Cook the buffalo burgers over medium-high heat to prevent them from becoming tough and dry.
3. Avoid overcooking the burgers to maintain their juiciness and tenderness.
4. Use a meat thermometer to ensure the buffalo burgers reach an internal temperature of 160°F for safe consumption.
5. Consider adding some fat to the patties, as buffalo meat is very lean and can easily dry out during cooking.
6. Top the burgers with your favorite toppings and enjoy alongside your preferred side dishes.

Indian tacos

Ingredients:

- 1 lb ground beef
- 1 packet taco seasoning
- 1 can refried beans
- 1 can diced tomatoes
- 1 cup shredded cheese
- 1/2 cup diced onion
- 1/4 cup chopped cilantro
- 4 Indian fry breads

Equipment:

1. Skillet
2. Wooden spoon
3. Spatula
4. Mixing bowl
5. Tongs

Methods:

Step 1: Preheat a skillet over medium heat and cook ground beef with taco seasoning until browned.
Step 2: In a separate bowl, mix flour, baking powder, salt, and water to form a dough.
Step 3: Divide dough into small balls and flatten into rounds.
Step 4: Heat oil in a skillet and fry dough rounds until golden brown and puffy.
Step 5: Top fried bread with cooked ground beef, lettuce, tomatoes, cheese, and any other desired toppings.
Step 6: Serve Indian tacos hot and enjoy the delicious flavors!

Helpful Tips:

1. Start by preparing the Indian taco dough - mix flour, baking powder, salt, and water until a soft dough forms.
2. Let the dough rest for about 30 minutes to allow the flavors to develop.
3. Divide the dough into equal portions and roll out into small discs.
4. Heat oil in a pan and fry the dough discs until they puff up and turn golden brown.
5. Prepare your favorite Indian taco fillings such as spicy ground meat, beans, cheese, onions, lettuce, and tomatoes.
6. Top the fried dough discs with your desired fillings and enjoy your delicious Indian tacos!

Blackberry cobbler

Ingredients:

- 4 cups fresh blackberries
- 1 cup sugar
- 1 cup flour
- 1/2 cup butter
- 1 tsp cinnamon
- 1 tsp vanilla extract
- 1/4 tsp salt

Equipment:

1. Mixing bowl
2. Whisk
3. Measuring cups
4. Baking dish
5. Spatula

Methods:

Step 1: Preheat the oven to 375°F.
Step 2: In a bowl, mix together 4 cups of fresh blackberries, 1 cup of sugar, and 1 tablespoon of lemon juice.
Step 3: Pour the blackberry mixture into a greased baking dish.
Step 4: In a separate bowl, mix together 1 cup of flour, 1 cup of sugar, 1 teaspoon of baking powder, and a pinch of salt.
Step 5: Cut in 1/2 cup of cold butter until the mixture resembles coarse crumbs.
Step 6: Sprinkle the flour mixture over the blackberries.
Step 7: Bake for 45-50 minutes, or until the topping is golden brown.
Step 8: Serve warm with vanilla ice cream. Enjoy your delicious blackberry cobbler!

Helpful Tips:

1. Preheat your oven to 375°F and gather all your ingredients.
2. In a large mixing bowl, combine fresh blackberries, sugar, and a squeeze of lemon juice.
3. Spread the blackberry mixture evenly in a baking dish.
4. In a separate bowl, mix together flour, sugar, baking powder, and a pinch of salt for the cobbler topping.
5. Cut in chilled butter using a pastry cutter until the mixture resembles coarse crumbs.
6. Stir in milk until just combined, being careful not to overmix.
7. Drop spoonfuls of the cobbler topping over the blackberry mixture.
8. Bake for about 45 minutes or until the cobbler topping is golden brown.
9. Enjoy warm with a scoop of vanilla ice cream!

Elk steak

Ingredients:

- 4 elk steaks
- 2 tbsp olive oil
- Salt and pepper to taste
- 1 tsp garlic powder
- 1 tsp paprika
- 1 tsp dried thyme

Equipment:

1. Skillet
2. Knife
3. Cutting board
4. Tongs
5. Baking sheet
6. Meat thermometer

Methods:

Step 1: Preheat your grill or skillet over medium-high heat.
Step 2: Season the elk steaks with salt, pepper, and any other desired seasonings.
Step 3: Place the steaks on the grill or skillet and cook for about 4-5 minutes per side for medium-rare.
Step 4: Use a meat thermometer to check for doneness - the internal temperature should reach 130-135°F for medium-rare.
Step 5: Remove the steaks from the heat and let them rest for 5 minutes before slicing and serving.
Step 6: Enjoy your perfectly cooked elk steak with your favorite side dishes.

Helpful Tips:

1. Allow the elk steak to come to room temperature before cooking.
2. Season the steak well with salt, pepper, and any other desired seasonings.
3. Preheat your cooking surface, whether it's a grill, stovetop, or oven, to a high heat.
4. Sear the elk steak on each side for a few minutes to lock in the juices.
5. Lower the heat and continue to cook the steak to your desired level of doneness.
6. Let the elk steak rest for a few minutes before slicing and serving.
7. Consider marinating the elk steak beforehand for added flavor.
8. Avoid overcooking the elk steak to prevent it from becoming tough.
9. Enjoy your delicious elk steak with your favorite side dishes.

Corn fritters

Ingredients:

- 1 cup of corn kernels
- 1/2 cup of flour
- 1 egg
- 1/4 cup of milk
- Salt and pepper to taste

Equipment:

1. Mixing bowl
2. Whisk
3. Frying pan
4. Spatula
5. Tongs

Methods:

Step 1: In a large bowl, combine 1 cup of cornmeal, 1/2 cup of flour, 1 teaspoon of baking powder, and 1/2 teaspoon of salt.
Step 2: Stir in 1 beaten egg, 1/2 cup of milk, and 1/4 cup of melted butter until well combined.
Step 3: Fold in 1 cup of fresh or canned corn kernels and 1/4 cup of chopped green onions.
Step 4: Heat oil in a skillet over medium heat.
Step 5: Drop spoonfuls of the batter into the hot oil and cook until golden brown on both sides.
Step 6: Drain on paper towels and serve hot with your favorite dipping sauce. Enjoy!

Helpful Tips:

1. Mix together fresh corn kernels, flour, eggs, milk, and seasonings in a bowl.
2. Heat oil in a skillet over medium heat.
3. Drop spoonfuls of the corn mixture into the hot oil.
4. Cook the fritters for 2-3 minutes on each side until they are golden brown.
5. Remove the fritters from the skillet and drain on a paper towel.
6. Serve the corn fritters hot with your favorite dipping sauce or toppings.
7. You can add chopped jalapenos or cheese to the corn mixture for extra flavor.
8. Make sure to season the fritters well with salt and pepper before cooking.

Sassafras tea

Ingredients:

- 4 cups water
- 4 teaspoons sassafras root bark
- 1/4 cup honey
- 1 cinnamon stick

Equipment:

1. Knife
2. Cutting board
3. Pot
4. Pan
5. Spoon
6. Tongs

Methods:

Step 1: Start by collecting a few fresh sassafras roots, preferably in the spring or fall when the sap is flowing.
Step 2: Scrub the roots clean under running water to remove any dirt or debris.
Step 3: Cut the roots into small pieces to release their flavor.
Step 4: Boil a pot of water and add the chopped sassafras roots.
Step 5: Let the mixture simmer for about 10-15 minutes to extract the flavors from the roots.
Step 6: Strain the liquid to remove the roots and any remaining particles.
Step 7: Pour the sassafras tea into a cup and enjoy hot or cold. Add honey or lemon for extra flavor if desired.

Helpful Tips:

1. Start by harvesting fresh sassafras root or buying dried, organic sassafras bark from a reputable source.
2. Wash and scrub the root thoroughly before chopping it into small pieces.
3. Boil water and add the chopped sassafras root or bark, simmering for around 20 minutes.
4. Strain the liquid through a fine mesh strainer to remove any debris.
5. Sweeten with honey or sugar to taste, and add a splash of lemon juice for a pop of acidity.
6. Enjoy your homemade sassafras tea hot or cold, and experiment with different flavor additions like cinnamon or ginger.

Maple bacon

Ingredients:

- 16 slices of bacon
- 4 tablespoons of maple syrup

Equipment:

1. Whisk
2. Mixing bowl
3. Frying pan
4. Chef's knife
5. Wooden spatula

Methods:

Step 1: Preheat your oven to 400°F.
Step 2: Line a baking sheet with aluminum foil and place a wire rack on top.
Step 3: Lay out strips of bacon on the wire rack.
Step 4: Brush each strip with maple syrup.
Step 5: Place the baking sheet in the preheated oven for 15-20 minutes, or until the bacon is crispy.
Step 6: Remove from oven and let cool for a few minutes.
Step 7: Enjoy your delicious maple bacon as a side dish or topping for your favorite breakfast foods.

Helpful Tips:

1. Start by selecting high-quality, thick-cut bacon for the best flavor.
2. Cook the bacon in a skillet over medium heat to ensure even cooking.
3. Add a touch of maple syrup to the bacon while it's cooking for a sweet and savory flavor.

4. Be careful not to overcook the bacon, as it can become tough and chewy.
5. Consider adding chopped pecans or walnuts to the bacon for added crunch and flavor.
6. Serve the maple bacon hot and crispy as a delicious breakfast side dish or as a topping for salads and sandwiches.

Wild greens salad

Ingredients:

- 8 cups mix of wild greens
- 1/2 cup cherry tomatoes
- 1/4 cup sliced almonds
- 1/4 cup crumbled feta cheese
- 1/4 cup balsamic vinaigrette

Equipment:

1. Mixing bowl
2. Salad tongs
3. Cutting board
4. Knife
5. Colander

Methods:

Step 1: Start by thoroughly washing the wild greens in a large bowl of cold water to remove any dirt or debris.
Step 2: Dry the greens completely using a salad spinner or by patting them with a clean kitchen towel.
Step 3: Tear the greens into bite-sized pieces and place them in a large salad bowl.
Step 4: Add your choice of additional vegetables or toppings, such as cherry tomatoes, cucumbers, and radishes.
Step 5: Drizzle with your favorite dressing, such as balsamic vinaigrette or lemon tahini.
Step 6: Toss the salad gently to combine all the ingredients and serve immediately. Enjoy your fresh and nutritious wild greens salad!

Helpful Tips:

1. Wash the wild greens thoroughly to remove any dirt or debris.
2. Use a variety of wild greens for flavor and texture, such as dandelion greens, arugula, and watercress.
3. Be mindful of any bitter flavors in the wild greens and balance them with sweet or acidic ingredients like fruits or vinaigrettes.
4. Add a protein element like grilled chicken or tofu to make the salad more filling.
5. Experiment with different toppings like nuts, seeds, or crumbled cheese for added crunch and flavor.
6. Dress the salad lightly with a simple vinaigrette to let the flavors of the wild greens shine through.

Bison ribs

Ingredients:

- 2 lbs Bison ribs
- 1 cup BBQ sauce
- 1/2 cup brown sugar
- 1 tbsp garlic powder
- Salt and pepper to taste

Equipment:

1. Knife
2. Cutting board
3. Tongs
4. Grill
5. Saucepan

Methods:

Step 1: Preheat your grill to medium-high heat.
Step 2: Season your bison ribs with salt, pepper, and any other desired seasonings.
Step 3: Place the ribs on the grill and cook for 5-7 minutes per side, or until they reach your desired level of doneness.
Step 4: Brush the ribs with your favorite barbecue sauce and continue to cook for an additional 2-3 minutes per side.
Step 5: Remove the ribs from the grill and let them rest for a few minutes before serving.
Step 6: Enjoy your delicious and tender bison ribs with your favorite side dishes!

Helpful Tips:

1. Begin by seasoning the bison ribs with a dry rub or marinade of your choice.
2. Preheat your grill to a medium-high heat and oil the grates to prevent sticking.
3. Place the bison ribs on the grill and cook for about 20-30 minutes per side, depending on the thickness of the ribs.
4. Use a meat thermometer to ensure the ribs reach an internal temperature of 140-160°F for medium-rare to medium doneness.
5. Let the bison ribs rest for a few minutes before serving to allow the juices to redistribute.
6. Serve with your favorite BBQ sauce or garnishes for added flavor. Enjoy!

Sunflower seed butter cookies

Ingredients:

- 1 cup sunflower seed butter
- 1/2 cup sugar
- 1 egg
- 1/2 tsp baking soda
- 1/4 tsp salt
- 1/2 cup chocolate chips

Equipment:

1. Mixing bowl
2. Baking sheet
3. Cookie scoop
4. Silicone spatula
5. Wire cooling rack

Methods:

Step 1: Preheat your oven to 350°F (180°C) and line a baking sheet with parchment paper.
Step 2: In a large mixing bowl, cream together 1 cup of sunflower seed butter, 1/2 cup of sugar, and 1/4 cup of brown sugar.
Step 3: Add in 1 egg and 1 teaspoon of vanilla extract, mixing until well combined.
Step 4: In a separate bowl, whisk together 1 cup of all-purpose flour, 1/2 teaspoon of baking soda, and a pinch of salt.
Step 5: Gradually add the dry ingredients to the wet ingredients, mixing until a dough forms.
Step 6: Roll the dough into small balls and place them on the prepared baking sheet.
Step 7: Flatten each ball with a fork and bake for 10-12 minutes, or until

the edges are golden brown.
Step 8: Allow the cookies to cool on the baking sheet before transferring to a wire rack to cool completely. Enjoy your sunflower seed butter cookies!

Helpful Tips:

1. Use creamy Sunflower seed butter for a smoother texture in your cookies.
2. Make sure to mix the Sunflower seed butter well with the other wet ingredients to avoid clumping.
3. Add extra flour if the dough is too sticky to handle.
4. Chill the dough in the refrigerator for at least 30 minutes before baking to prevent spreading.
5. Press down on the cookie dough with a fork to create a crisscross pattern for traditional peanut butter cookie look.
6. Watch the cookies carefully while baking as Sunflower seed butter can easily burn.
7. Let the cookies cool completely on a wire rack before serving.

Wild onion soup

Ingredients:

- 4 cups wild onions
- 6 cups vegetable broth
- 1/2 cup heavy cream
- Salt and pepper to taste

Equipment:

1. Saucepan
2. Wooden spoon
3. Ladle
4. Chef's knife
5. Cutting board

Methods:

Step 1: Gather ingredients including wild onions, vegetable broth, butter, flour, salt, pepper, and cream.
Step 2: Wash and chop the wild onions, separating the white and green parts.
Step 3: In a large pot, melt butter over medium heat and add in the white parts of the wild onions.
Step 4: Cook until the onions are softened, then sprinkle in flour and stir to create a roux.
Step 5: Slowly pour in the vegetable broth while stirring constantly to avoid lumps.
Step 6: Add in the green parts of the wild onions, salt, and pepper. Simmer for 15 minutes.
Step 7: Stir in cream and serve hot. Enjoy your wild onion soup!

Helpful Tips:

1. Start by sautéing chopped wild onions in a pot with butter or oil until they are fragrant and soft.
2. Add in chicken or vegetable broth and bring to a simmer.
3. Season with salt, pepper, and any other desired herbs or spices.
4. Let the soup simmer for at least 20-30 minutes to allow the flavors to meld together.
5. For a creamier texture, you can blend the soup with an immersion blender or in a traditional blender.
6. Serve the soup hot garnished with a sprinkle of chopped wild onions.
7. Enjoy with crusty bread or a side salad for a complete meal.

Elk roast

Ingredients:

- 2 lbs elk roast
- 1 onion, sliced
- 2 cloves garlic, minced
- 1/2 cup beef broth
- Salt and pepper to taste

Equipment:

1. Knife
2. Cutting board
3. Skillet
4. Tongs
5. Roasting pan

Methods:

Step 1: Preheat your oven to 325°F.
Step 2: Season your elk roast generously with salt, pepper, and any other desired herbs or spices.
Step 3: Heat a large skillet over medium-high heat and sear the elk roast on all sides until browned.
Step 4: Place the roast in a roasting pan and cook in the preheated oven for about 20 minutes per pound, or until a meat thermometer reads 135°F for medium-rare.
Step 5: Let the roast rest for 10-15 minutes before slicing.
Step 6: Serve the elk roast with your favorite sides and enjoy!

Helpful Tips:

1. Trim excess fat off the elk roast to prevent a gamey flavor.
2. Marinate the elk roast in a mixture of olive oil, herbs, and spices for at least 24 hours.
3. Preheat the oven to 325°F before cooking the elk roast.
4. Sear the roast in a hot skillet before transferring it to the oven to lock in juices.
5. Use a meat thermometer to ensure the roast reaches an internal temperature of 135-140°F for medium rare.
6. Let the elk roast rest for at least 10 minutes before slicing to allow the juices to redistribute.
7. Serve the elk roast with a flavorful sauce or gravy to enhance the taste.

Acorn squash soup

Ingredients:

- 1 acorn squash
- 1 onion
- 2 cloves garlic
- 4 cups vegetable broth
- 1/2 tsp thyme
- 1/2 tsp nutmeg
- Salt and pepper to taste

Equipment:

1. Chef's knife
2. Cutting board
3. Soup pot
4. Immersion blender
5. Ladle

Methods:

Step 1: Preheat oven to 400°F.
Step 2: Cut the acorn squash in half and scoop out the seeds.
Step 3: Place the squash halves cut-side down on a baking sheet.
Step 4: Roast in the oven for 45-50 minutes, or until tender.
Step 5: Allow the squash to cool, then scoop out the flesh and discard the skins.
Step 6: In a large pot, sauté onions and garlic until translucent.
Step 7: Add the squash flesh, vegetable broth, and seasonings to the pot.
Step 8: Simmer for 20 minutes.
Step 9: Blend the soup until smooth using an immersion blender.
Step 10: Serve hot and enjoy!

Helpful Tips:

1. Start by roasting the acorn squash in the oven to bring out its natural sweetness.
2. Add diced onions, garlic, and celery to a pot with some olive oil for a flavorful base.
3. Use vegetable or chicken broth as your soup base for added flavor.
4. Blend the roasted acorn squash with the sautéed vegetables and broth until smooth and creamy.
5. Add a touch of heavy cream or coconut milk for extra richness.
6. Season with salt, pepper, and your favorite herbs or spices.
7. Top with toasted pumpkin seeds or a drizzle of olive oil before serving.

Blueberry pancakes

Ingredients:

- 1 cup of flour
- 1 tbsp of sugar
- 1 tsp of baking powder
- 1/2 tsp of salt
- 1 cup of milk
- 1 egg
- 1 cup of blueberries

Equipment:

1. Frying pan
2. Spatula
3. Mixing bowl
4. Whisk
5. Griddle
6. Measuring cup

Methods:

Step 1: In a large mixing bowl, whisk together 1 1/2 cups of all-purpose flour, 3 1/2 teaspoons of baking powder, 1 teaspoon of salt, and 1 tablespoon of sugar.
Step 2: In a separate bowl, whisk together 1 1/4 cups of milk, 1 egg, and 3 tablespoons of melted butter.
Step 3: Combine the wet and dry ingredients, stirring until just combined.
Step 4: Gently fold in 1 cup of fresh blueberries.
Step 5: Heat a non-stick skillet or griddle over medium heat and lightly grease with butter.
Step 6: Pour 1/4 cup of batter onto the skillet for each pancake and cook until bubbles form on the surface.

Step 7: Flip and cook for an additional 2-3 minutes.
Step 8: Serve warm with maple syrup and additional blueberries, if desired.
Enjoy your delicious blueberry pancakes!

Helpful Tips:

1. Start by whisking together dry ingredients - flour, sugar, baking powder, and salt.
2. In a separate bowl, mix together wet ingredients - eggs, milk, and melted butter.
3. Gently fold wet ingredients into the dry mixture until just combined.
4. Gently fold in fresh blueberries.
5. Heat a non-stick skillet over medium heat and add a bit of butter or oil.
6. Pour batter onto the skillet in small circles and cook until bubbles form on the surface.
7. Flip pancakes and cook for another minute or until golden brown.
8. Serve with maple syrup and extra fresh blueberries on top. Enjoy!

Bison roast

Ingredients:

- 2 lb bison roast
- 1 onion, sliced
- 2 cloves garlic, minced
- 1 cup beef broth
- Salt and pepper to taste

Equipment:

1. Chef's knife
2. Cutting board
3. Roasting pan
4. Oven mitts
5. Meat thermometer

Methods:

Step 1: Preheat the oven to 325°F.
Step 2: Season the Bison roast with salt, pepper, and any desired herbs or spices.
Step 3: Heat a large skillet over medium-high heat and sear the Bison roast on all sides until browned.
Step 4: Place the seared roast on a roasting pan and insert a meat thermometer into the thickest part of the meat.
Step 5: Roast the Bison in the preheated oven until the internal temperature reaches 135°F for medium-rare or 145°F for medium.
Step 6: Remove the Bison roast from the oven and let it rest for 10-15 minutes before slicing and serving. Enjoy your delicious Bison roast!

Helpful Tips:

1. Choose a high-quality bison roast from a reputable source.
2. Marinate the roast for at least 6 hours to enhance flavor and tenderness.
3. Preheat your oven to 325°F (163°C) before cooking the roast.
4. Use a meat thermometer to ensure the internal temperature reaches at least 145°F (63°C) for medium-rare doneness.
5. Let the roast rest for 10-15 minutes after cooking to allow the juices to redistribute.
6. Serve with a savory gravy or sauce to enhance the flavor of the bison.
7. Slice the roast against the grain to ensure tenderness.
8. Enjoy your delicious and nutritious bison roast!

Parsnip mash

Ingredients:

- 4 parsnips
- 2 tbsp butter
- 1/4 cup milk
- Salt and pepper
- Chopped parsley (optional)
- Nutmeg powder

Equipment:

1. Knife
2. Cutting board
3. Saucepan
4. Wooden spoon
5. Potato masher

Methods:

Step 1: Peel and chop 4-5 parsnips into small pieces.
Step 2: Boil the parsnips in a pot with water and a pinch of salt for about 15-20 minutes, or until they are soft.
Step 3: Drain the parsnips and return them to the pot.
Step 4: Add a knob of butter and a splash of milk to the pot.
Step 5: Mash the parsnips until smooth using a potato masher or immersion blender.
Step 6: Season with salt and pepper to taste.
Step 7: Serve the parsnip mash as a delicious and creamy side dish. Enjoy!

Helpful Tips:

1. Peel and chop parsnips into small, uniform pieces for even cooking.
2. Boil parsnips in salted water until fork-tender, about 10-15 minutes.
3. Drain parsnips well to avoid watery mash.
4. Mash parsnips with a potato masher or blend in a food processor for a smoother texture.
5. Add butter, cream, or milk to the mash for added richness and creaminess.
6. Season with salt, pepper, and optional herbs like thyme or rosemary.
7. Consider adding roasted garlic or caramelized onions for extra flavor.
8. Serve hot as a side dish to accompany roasted meats or vegetables.

Duck confit

Ingredients:

- 4 duck legs
- 4 cloves garlic
- 2 tbsp salt
- 1 tsp black pepper
- 4 sprigs thyme
- 2 cups duck fat

Equipment:

1. Chef's knife
2. Cutting board
3. Dutch oven
4. Tongs
5. Whisk

Methods:

Step 1: Preheat the oven to 250°F.
Step 2: Season duck legs with salt, pepper, and any other desired herbs/spices.
Step 3: Place duck legs in a single layer in a deep baking dish.
Step 4: Add enough duck fat (or olive oil) to cover the duck legs.
Step 5: Cover the dish with foil and bake in the preheated oven for 2-3 hours.
Step 6: Remove foil and increase oven temperature to 400°F.
Step 7: Bake for an additional 15-20 minutes until the skin is crispy and browned.
Step 8: Serve hot and enjoy your delicious duck confit!

Helpful Tips:

1. Use duck legs or thighs for the best flavor and texture.
2. Salt the duck and let it cure in the fridge for 24-48 hours before cooking.
3. Rinse off the salt and pat the duck dry before cooking.
4. Cook the duck in its own fat or use a combination of duck fat and oil for extra richness.
5. Cook the duck slowly at a low temperature (around 180-200°F) for several hours until the meat is tender and falling off the bone.
6. Store the duck in the fat after cooking to keep it moist and flavorful.
7. Reheat the duck in a hot oven to crisp up the skin before serving.

Maple roasted turnips

Ingredients:

- 4 medium turnips
- 2 tbsp maple syrup
- 1 tbsp olive oil
- Salt and pepper to taste

Equipment:

1. Chef's knife
2. Cutting board
3. Mixing bowls
4. Roasting pan
5. Basting brush

Methods:

Step 1: Preheat the oven to 400°F.
Step 2: Peel and chop the turnips into bite-sized pieces.
Step 3: In a bowl, toss the turnips with olive oil, maple syrup, salt, and pepper.
Step 4: Spread the turnips out on a baking sheet in a single layer.
Step 5: Roast in the oven for about 25-30 minutes, or until the turnips are tender and slightly caramelized.
Step 6: Optional - sprinkle with fresh herbs like parsley or thyme before serving.
Step 7: Enjoy your delicious maple roasted turnips as a side dish or snack!

Helpful Tips:

1. Preheat your oven to 400°F.
2. Peel and dice your turnips into uniform pieces for even cooking.
3. Toss the turnips in olive oil, maple syrup, salt, and pepper in a bowl until well coated.
4. Spread the turnips out in a single layer on a baking sheet lined with parchment paper.
5. Roast in the oven for 25-30 minutes, flipping halfway through, until the turnips are caramelized and tender.
6. For extra flavor, sprinkle with fresh thyme or rosemary before serving.
7. Enjoy as a delicious side dish or add to salads or grain bowls for a tasty twist.

Wild rice porridge

Ingredients:

- 1 cup of wild rice
- 4 cups of water
- 1/4 cup of maple syrup
- 1/2 tsp of cinnamon

Equipment:

1. Pot
2. Wooden spoon
3. Whisk
4. Ladle
5. Measuring cup

Methods:

Step 1: Rinse 1 cup of wild rice under cold water.
Step 2: In a saucepan, bring 3 cups of water to a boil.
Step 3: Add the rinsed wild rice to the boiling water.
Step 4: Reduce heat to low, cover with a lid, and let simmer for 45-50 minutes.
Step 5: Stir occasionally to prevent sticking.
Step 6: In a separate saucepan, heat 1 cup of milk until warm.
Step 7: Once the wild rice is cooked, pour in the warm milk and stir well.
Step 8: Add honey, cinnamon, or any desired toppings before serving.
Step 9: Enjoy your delicious wild rice porridge!

Helpful Tips:

1. Rinse the wild rice before cooking to remove any debris.
2. Use a mixture of water and broth for added flavor.
3. Add in some vegetables such as carrots, onions, and celery for extra nutrients.
4. Consider using a slow cooker for a hands-off cooking experience.
5. Season with herbs and spices like thyme, sage, and garlic for a savory taste.
6. Stir occasionally to prevent sticking and ensure even cooking.
7. Add in protein sources like chicken or tofu for a balanced meal.
8. Serve with toppings like toasted nuts, dried fruit, or a drizzle of maple syrup for added texture and sweetness.

Squash soup

Ingredients:

- 1 butternut squash (2 lbs)
- 1 medium onion
- 1 quart vegetable broth
- 1/2 cup heavy cream

Equipment:

1. Blender
2. Saucepan
3. Immersion blender
4. Ladle
5. Knife

Methods:

Step 1: Preheat the oven to 400°F.
Step 2: Cut a medium-sized squash in half, remove the seeds, and place it face down on a baking sheet.
Step 3: Roast the squash in the oven for 45-60 minutes or until tender.
Step 4: In a large pot, sauté chopped onions and garlic in olive oil until soft.
Step 5: Scoop the cooked squash out of the skin and add it to the pot.
Step 6: Add vegetable broth, salt, pepper, and any desired herbs or spices.
Step 7: Simmer the soup for 10-15 minutes.
Step 8: Blend the soup until smooth.
Step 9: Serve hot and enjoy!

Helpful Tips:

1. Start by roasting the squash to enhance its natural sweetness and flavor.
2. Add aromatics like garlic, onions, and herbs to deepen the soup's flavor profile.
3. Use a high-quality broth or stock as the base for the soup for added richness.
4. Consider adding a touch of heat with a pinch of cayenne or red pepper flakes.
5. Blend the soup until smooth for a creamy texture, or leave some chunks for added texture.
6. Finish the soup with a swirl of cream, a dollop of yogurt, or a sprinkle of fresh herbs for a finishing touch.
7. Don't forget to season the soup with salt and pepper to taste before serving.

Bison chili

Ingredients:

- 2 lbs Bison
- 1 onion
- 2 cloves garlic
- 1 bell pepper
- 1 can diced tomatoes
- 1 can kidney beans
- 2 tbsp chili powder
- 1 tsp cumin
- Salt and pepper to taste

Equipment:

1. Skillet
2. Wooden spoon
3. Ladle
4. Knife
5. Cutting board

Methods:

Step 1: In a large pot, heat olive oil over medium heat.
Step 2: Add chopped onion and cook until translucent.
Step 3: Add diced bison meat and cook until browned.
Step 4: Stir in chili powder, cumin, and paprika.
Step 5: Pour in diced tomatoes, tomato sauce, and beef broth.
Step 6: Add kidney beans, corn, and bell peppers.
Step 7: Bring to a boil, then reduce heat and simmer for at least 30 minutes.
Step 8: Taste and adjust seasoning as needed with salt and pepper.

Step 9: Serve hot with toppings like shredded cheese, sour cream, and green onions. Enjoy your delicious bison chili!

Helpful Tips:

1. Start by browning the ground bison in a large pot over medium heat. Drain any excess fat.
2. Add diced onions, garlic, and bell peppers to the pot and cook until softened.
3. Stir in chili powder, cumin, and red pepper flakes for added heat.
4. Pour in crushed tomatoes, beef broth, and kidney beans.
5. Let the chili simmer for at least 30 minutes to allow the flavors to meld together.
6. Taste and adjust seasoning as needed with salt and pepper.
7. Serve hot with your favorite toppings like shredded cheese, sour cream, and chopped green onions.
8. Enjoy your hearty and flavorful bison chili!

Made in United States
Orlando, FL
09 April 2024